Maths

Age 7-8

Contents

Activities

Quick Tests

Paul Broadbent and Peter Patilla

Number sequences

Look at the difference between numbers in a **sequence**.

This will help you to spot any **patterns**.

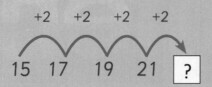 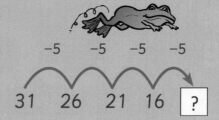

+2	+2	+2	+2

15   17   19   21   ?

The next number is 23.

−5	−5	−5	−5

31   26   21   16   ?

The next number is 11.

1 Write the next three numbers in each sequence.

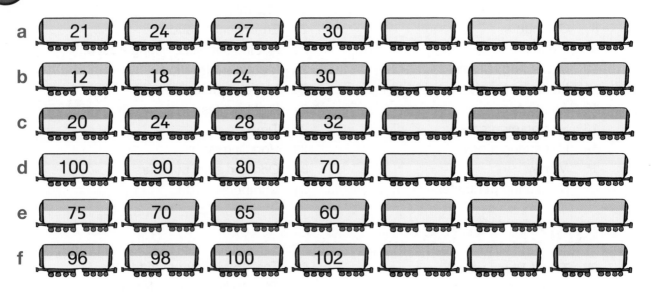

a 21 24 27 30

b 12 18 24 30

c 20 24 28 32

d 100 90 80 70

e 75 70 65 60

f 96 98 100 102

2 Continue the jumps. Write the next four new numbers in the sequence.

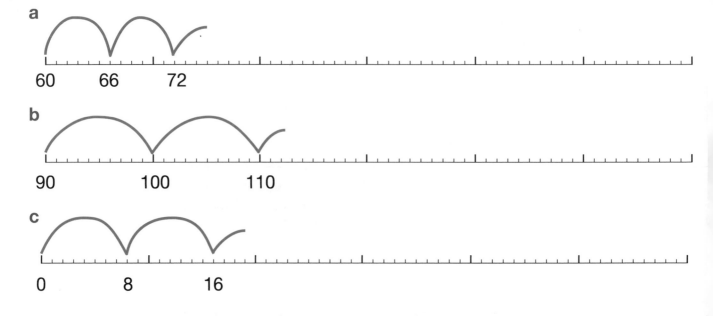

a 60 66 72

b 90 100 110

c 0 8 16

Place value

3-digit numbers are made from **hundreds, tens** and **ones**.

hundreds   tens   ones

436 = 400 + 30 + 6

The position of the digits 0 to 9 gives the value of the number.

1 **Write the missing numbers.**

a 482 = 400 + ☐ + 2

b 745 = 700 + 40 + ☐

c 193 = ☐ + 90 + ☐

d 216 = 200 + ☐ + ☐

e 552 = ☐ + ☐ + 2

f 324 = ☐ + 20 + ☐

g 627 = ☐ + ☐ + ☐

h 813 = ☐ + ☐ + ☐

i 945 = ☐ + ☐ + ☐

j 799 = ☐ + ☐ + ☐

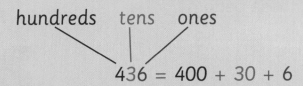

2 **Read the number on the abacus. Add the number below and write the new number.**

a

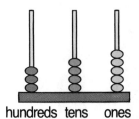

hundreds tens ones

Add 5 ☐

b

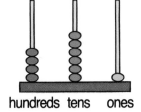

hundreds tens ones

Add 9 ☐

c

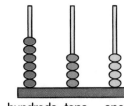

hundreds tens ones

Add 60 ☐

Addition and subtraction

If you learn the addition and subtraction facts to 20, they can help you to learn other facts. Look at these patterns.

$$4 + 9 = 13$$

$$40 + 90 = 130$$

$$400 + 900 = 1300$$

$$15 - 8 = 7$$

$$150 - 80 = 70$$

$$1500 - 800 = 700$$

$5 + 7 = 12$

1 **Write the answers to these questions.**

a 7 + 5 = ☐
70 + 50 = ☐
700 + 500 = ☐

b 9 + 6 = ☐
90 + 60 = ☐
900 + 600 = ☐

c 4 + 11 = ☐
40 + 110 = ☐
400 + 1100 = ☐

d 13 − 6 = ☐
130 − 60 = ☐
1300 − 600 = ☐

e 15 − 7 = ☐
150 − 70 = ☐
1500 − 700 = ☐

f 18 − 9 = ☐
180 − 90 = ☐
1800 − 900 = ☐

g 180 − 60 = ☐

h 800 + 500 = ☐

i 1700 − 400 = ☐

j 1200 + 600 = ☐

k 150 + 90 = ☐

l 130 − 90 = ☐

m 800 + 800 = ☐

2 **Circle touching pairs of numbers that total 100. The pairs can be vertical or horizontal. You should find ten pairs.**

34	51	59	41	76	82	38	62
66	75	25	65	24	47	53	77
91	19	72	83	17	45	96	13
24	81	74	56	35	55	48	52

Subtraction

When you subtract numbers, decide whether to use a **mental method**, or whether you need to use the **written method**.

Mental method 92 − 57 = 35

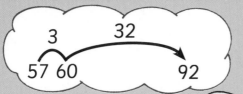

3   32

57 60   92

57 on to 60 is 3

60 on to 92 is 32

32 add 3 is 35

Written method 143 − 86 = 57

4   10   43

86 90   100   143

Count on from 86 in steps
4 + 10 + 43 = 57

These both use a number line to work out the answers.

1 Use the number line method for these.

a 74 − 38 = ☐

38   74

c 93 − 57 = ☐

57   93

e 152 − 76 = ☐

76   152

b 81 − 46 = ☐

46   81

d 125 − 87 = ☐

87   125

f 164 − 95 = ☐

95   164

2 Choose a method to work out the differences between these pairs of weights.

a

Difference: ☐ kg

b

Difference: ☐ kg

c

Difference: ☐ kg

d

Difference: ☐ kg

e
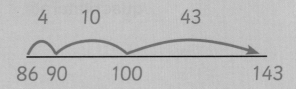

Difference: ☐ kg

f

Difference: ☐ kg

2-D shapes

 3-sided shapes are **triangles**.

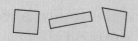 4-sided shapes are **quadrilaterals**.

 5-sided shapes are **pentagons**.

 6-sided shapes are **hexagons**.

 circle

 semi-circle

 oval

1 Cross the odd one out in each set. Name each set of shapes.

a

_____

c

_____

b

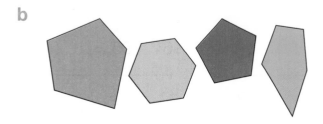

_____

d

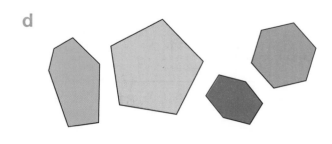

_____

2 There are two shapes in this box that are not in the red box. Colour the two shapes.

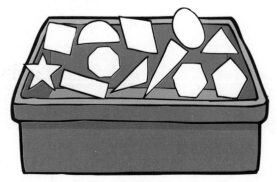

There are two shapes in this box that are not in the blue box. Colour the two shapes.

Ordering numbers

When you put 3-digit numbers in **order**, look at the **hundreds** first, then the **tens** and then the **ones** digit.

785 grams is heavier than 758 grams.

785 g
758 g   8 tens is more than 5 tens.

1 Write these in order, smallest first.

a
207 cm   87 cm
137 cm
170 cm
107 cm

b
225 ml 308 ml
340 ml
275 ml 272 ml

c
£1 and 70p
£1 and 95p
£1 and 38p
£2 and 5p
£1 and 9p

d
802 m   635 m
525 m
610 m   608 m

2 These number cards were in order. Colour the two cards that have been changed over.

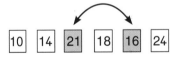

| 10 | 14 | 21 | 18 | 16 | 24 |

a | 7 | 11 | 15 | 19 | 17 | 16 | 21 |

b | 23 | 28 | 34 | 39 | 48 | 42 | 56 |

c | 63 | 52 | 57 | 36 | 71 | 74 | 82 |

d | 108 | 114 | 123 | 184 | 215 | 212 | 206 |

Calendars

A calendar shows **dates**.

It usually shows:

- the day
- the date
- the month
- the year.

Friday
8th
October
2004

There are 12 months in a year.

JANUARY	FEBRUARY	MARCH	APRIL
MAY	JUNE	JULY	AUGUST
SEPTEMBER	OCTOBER	NOVEMBER	DECEMBER

1 Use this calendar to help answer these questions.

a What is the month? _____

b On which day is the 22nd? _____

c What date is the
second Friday? _____

d What date is one week after
the 19th? _____

e On which day is the
30th April? _____

f On which day is the
2nd June? _____

May 2004

S	M	T	W	T	F	S
						1
2	3	4	5	6	7	8
9	10	11	12	13	14	15
16	17	18	19	20	21	22
23	24	25	26	27	28	29
30	31					

2 Learn this method for remembering the number of days in each month.

a Hold your hands in front of you,
so you can see your knuckles.

b Start with January from the left
knuckle of your little finger.

c Move to the right, with February in
the gap, March the next knuckle
and so on.

d All the knuckle months have
31 days.

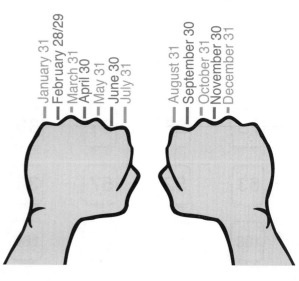

January 31
February 28/29
March 31
April 30
May 31
June 30
July 31
August 31
September 30
October 31
November 30
December 31

Fractions

Fractions show the number of **equal parts** of a whole.

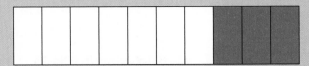

This shows three-tenths or $\frac{3}{10}$. It is one whole divided into ten equal parts. Three parts are shaded.

$\frac{2}{3}$ of 6 = 4

1 Colour the shapes to show each fraction.

a $\frac{3}{4}$

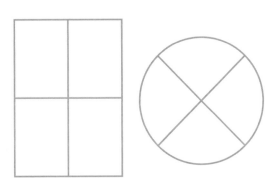

c $\frac{3}{5}$

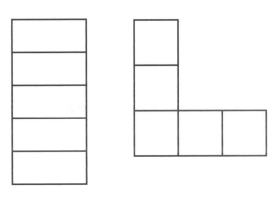

b $\frac{2}{3}$

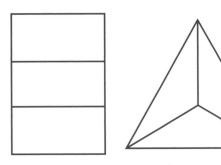

d $\frac{7}{10}$

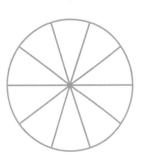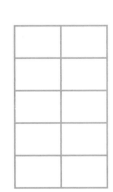

2 Write the answers to these.

a $\frac{3}{4}$ of 12 =

b $\frac{1}{8}$ of 16 =

c $\frac{3}{10}$ of 40 =

d $\frac{2}{3}$ of 15 =

e $\frac{4}{5}$ of 30 =

f $\frac{1}{12}$ of 24 =

g $\frac{3}{4}$ of 20 =

h $\frac{2}{3}$ of 21 =

9

Measuring length

Practise measuring things to the nearest $\frac{1}{2}$ centimetre.

An **estimate** is a rough answer without measuring.

This line is about $5\frac{1}{2}$ cm long.

If you estimated this line to be about 5 or 6 cm, that is a very good estimate.

1 Use a ruler to measure each length to the nearest half centimetre.

a [____] cm

b [____] cm

c [____] cm

d [____] cm

e [____] cm

f [____] cm

2 Use a ruler to draw a line for each measurement.

a 5 cm →

b 8 cm →

c 10 cm →

Multiplication facts

Try to learn these **multiplication** tables.

×	0	1	2	3	4	5	6	7	8	9	10	11	12
2	0	2	4	6	8	10	12	14	16	18	20	22	24
3	0	3	6	9	12	15	18	21	24	27	30	33	36
4	0	4	8	12	16	20	24	28	32	36	40	44	48
5	0	5	10	15	20	25	30	35	40	45	50	55	60
8	0	8	16	24	32	40	48	56	64	72	80	88	96
10	0	10	20	30	40	50	60	70	80	90	100	110	120
11	0	11	22	33	44	55	66	77	88	99	110	121	132
12	0	12	24	36	48	60	72	84	96	108	120	132	144

$4 \times 5 = 20$

$5 \times 4 = 20$

The order does not matter.

1 **Answer these as quickly as you can.**

a 10×2 =

10×7 =

10×8 =

10×10 =

3×10 =

9×10 =

c 2×2 =

2×7 =

2×8 =

6×2 =

3×2 =

9×2 =

e 4×12 =

7×8 =

11×5 =

3×4 =

3×8 =

12×8 =

b 5×2 =

5×7 =

5×8 =

6×5 =

3×5 =

9×5 =

d 6×8 =

4×7 =

4×8 =

11×4 =

3×12 =

8×8 =

2 **Answer these. Use the code to find the name of two cities in Scotland.**

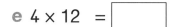

a 4×5 5×5 7×3 10×2 6×4 8×3

☐ ☐ ☐ ☐ ☐ ☐

b 4×6 2×10 4×4 3×7 5×7 5×5 3×10 8×5 6×3

☐ ☐ ☐ ☐ ☐ ☐ ☐ ☐ ☐

Addition

When you add numbers, decide whether to use a **mental method**, or whether you need to use the **written method**.

Mental method 53 + 48

Example

> 53 add 50 is 103
> Take away 2 is 101

> 53 add 40 is 93
> 93 add 8 is 101

Written method 156 + 75

Example

```
  1 5 6
+   7 5
  ─────
  2 3 1
  1 1
```

Add the ones (6 + 5)

Then the tens
(50 + 70 + 10)

Then the hundreds
(100 + 100)

1 Use your own methods to add these. Colour the star if you used a mental method.

a 51 + 43 = ☐ ☆   e 91 + 74 = ☐ ☆   i 88 + 83 = ☐ ☆

b 38 + 63 = ☐ ☆   f 57 + 69 = ☐ ☆   j 124 + 132 = ☐ ☆

c 29 + 35 = ☐ ☆   g 37 + 94 = ☐ ☆   k 146 + 105 = ☐ ☆

d 86 + 62 = ☐ ☆   h 75 + 66 = ☐ ☆   l 135 + 166 = ☐ ☆

2 Answer these.

a
```
  3 8 6
+   5 8
──────
```

c
```
  5 4 6
+   7 4
──────
```

e
```
  6 7 6
+   7 8
──────
```

b
```
  2 7 4
+   8 1
──────
```

d
```
  9 1 4
+   8 7
──────
```

f
```
  7 2 7
+   8 3
──────
```

> 386
> +58

Sorting diagrams

Compare these **sorting diagrams** for numbers to 10.

Venn diagram

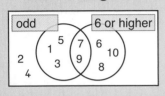

Carroll diagram

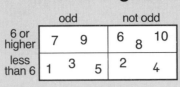

Tree diagram

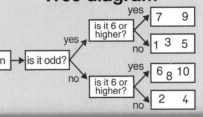

1 Draw these shapes in the correct parts of each diagram.

a

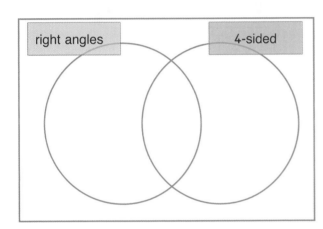

b

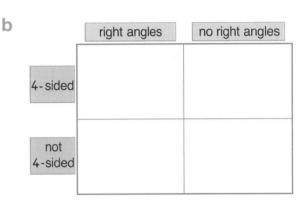

2 This diagram sorts numbers.

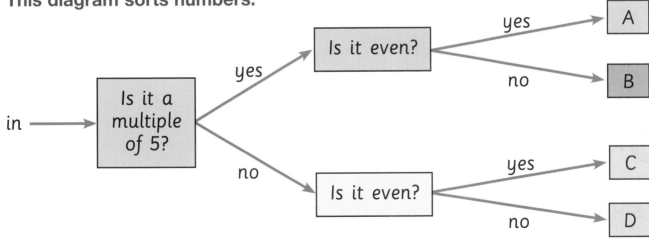

Into which boxes will these numbers be sorted?

a 27 → ☐ b 18 → ☐ c 40 → ☐ d 25 → ☐ e 30 → ☐

Measuring mass

We find the **mass** or **weight** of an object using scales.

We weigh in **grams** and **kilograms**.

1000 grams = 1 kilogram

1000 g = 1 kg

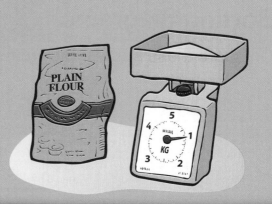

1 Write the mass shown on each of these.

a
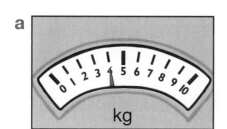
kg
☐ kg

b
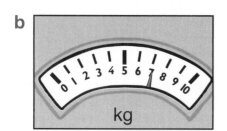
kg
☐ kg

c
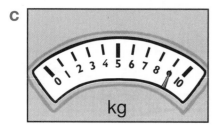
kg
☐ kg

d
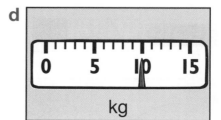
kg
☐ kg

e
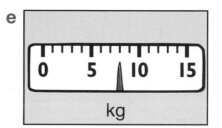
kg
☐ kg

f
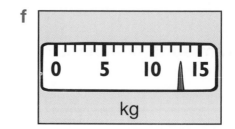
kg
☐ kg

2 Answer these questions.

a How many 100 g weights balance 1 kg? ☐

b How many 500 g weights balance 1 kg? ☐

c How many 200 g weights balance 1 kg? ☐

d How many 250 g weights balance 1 kg? ☐

e How many 50 g weights balance 500 g? ☐

Money

There are **100 pence in £1**.

£1	=	100p
£2 and 60p	=	260p
£1 and 35p	=	135p
£3 and 9p	=	309p

1 Write the coin values in the circles to show the fewest number of coins you would give for items at these prices.

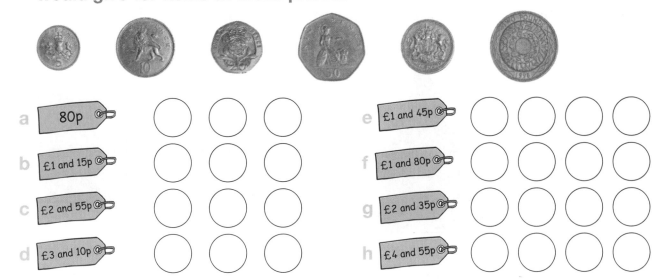

a 80p ◯ ◯ ◯

b £1 and 15p ◯ ◯ ◯

c £2 and 55p ◯ ◯ ◯

d £3 and 10p ◯ ◯ ◯

e £1 and 45p ◯ ◯ ◯ ◯

f £1 and 80p ◯ ◯ ◯ ◯

g £2 and 35p ◯ ◯ ◯ ◯

h £4 and 55p ◯ ◯ ◯ ◯

2 Draw coins in the empty purse. It should contain half the number of coins as the other purse but the same total amount of money.

a

Total: 70p

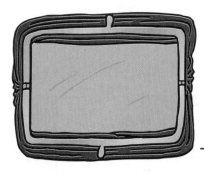

Total: 70p

b

Total: £ ☐ and ☐ p

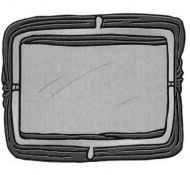

Total: £ ☐ and ☐ p

Measuring perimeter

The perimeter of a shape is the **distance all around the edge**.

The perimeter of this triangle is
3 cm + 4 cm + 5 cm = 12 cm

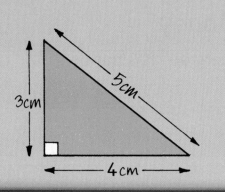

1 Use a ruler to measure the perimeter of each shape.

a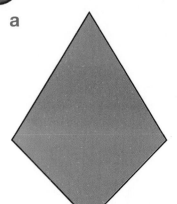

b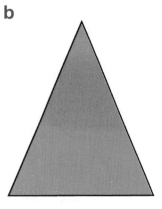

c

d

Perimeter =

_____

Perimeter =

_____

Perimeter =

_____

Perimeter =

_____

2 Write the perimeter of each rectangle.

a Perimeter: [ ] cm

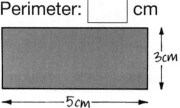

b Perimeter: [ ] cm

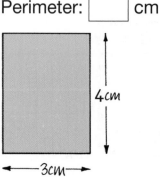

c Perimeter: [ ] cm

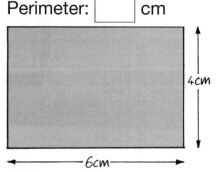

d Perimeter: [ ] cm

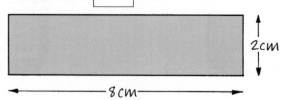

e Perimeter: [ ] cm

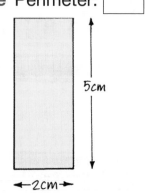

Addition and subtraction problems

Here are some **addition** words:

altogether more add
total plus sum

Here are some **subtraction** words:

subtract leaves minus
take away difference less

1 Answer these questions.

a What is the sum of
30 and 50?

b What is the total of the
first four odd numbers?

c What is the difference
between 70 and 110?

d What is 16 more than 25?

e Which number is 9
less than 22?

f What is 45 take away 20?

g What is the total of
80, 90, 100?

h What is 500 minus 150?

2 Try these money problems.

a Circle the **three** presents that can
be bought for exactly £1.

b Join the **four** presents that can be
bought for exactly £1 and 50p.

Symmetry

A **line of symmetry** shows where a **mirror line** could be drawn.

One half of the shape is a **reflection** of the other half.

These have 1 line of symmetry.   These have 2 lines of symmetry.

1 Draw the line or lines of symmetry on each shape.

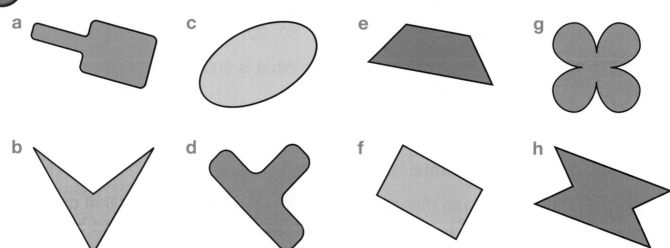

a

c

e

g

b

d

f

h

2 Draw and colour the reflection of each shape.

a

b

18

Measuring capacity

We measure the capacity of containers in **millilitres** and **litres**.

1000 millilitres = 1 litre

1000 ml = 1 l

You can read the scale on the side of a jug carefully to work out the capacity.

---

1 Write how much liquid is in each container.

a

[ ] ml

c

[ ] ml

e

[ ] ml

b

[ ] ml

d

[ ] ml

f

[ ] ml

---

2 Answer these.

a 1 litre = [ ] ml

b $\frac{1}{2}$ litre = [ ] ml

c $\frac{1}{4}$ litre = [ ] ml

d $\frac{1}{10}$ litre = [ ] ml

e How many 200 ml bottles will fill a 1 litre jug? [ ]

f How many 50 ml bottles will fill a 500 ml jug? [ ]

Division

Sometimes when you **divide** there is an amount **left over**.

This is called a **remainder**.

If you wanted to share 7 sweets between 3 people, they would each have 2 sweets with 1 left over.

7 ÷ 3 = 2 remainder 1

1 Group these and write the answers.

a    13 ÷ 2 = ☐ remainder ☐

b    22 ÷ 5 = ☐ remainder ☐

c 17 ÷ 3 = ☐ remainder ☐

d    15 ÷ 4 = ☐ remainder ☐

e    16 ÷ 5 = ☐ remainder ☐

f    20 ÷ 3 = ☐ remainder ☐

2 Draw lines to join these to the correct remainder.

remainder

1

2

3

4

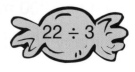

3-D shapes

Learn the names of these shapes.

cube   cone   pyramid   sphere

cuboid   cylinder   prism

Prisms have:
- two end faces that are the same
- rectangular sides.

If you slice a prism into equal lengths, all the slices will be the same shape and size.

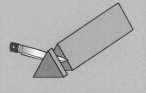

1 Write how many faces these shapes have. Name each shape.

a

☐ faces

_____

c
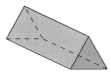
☐ faces

_____

e
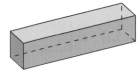
☐ faces

_____

b

☐ faces

_____

d
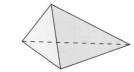
☐ faces

_____

f

☐ faces

_____

2 Write the letter for each shape in the correct part of the Carroll diagram.

a

b

c

	prism	not a prism
1 or more triangle faces		
no triangle faces		

d

e

g

f

Mental addition

Adding **larger numbers** can be easy if you are quick at adding **small numbers**.

$$4 + 3 = 7$$
$$40 + 30 = 70$$
$$45 + 30 = 75$$

Adding numbers such as 19, 29, 39 … can be worked out like this.

$$45 + 29$$
$$\downarrow$$
$$45 + 30 - 1 = 75 - 1 = 74$$

1 Answer these.

a 40 + 40 = ☐

46 + 40 = ☐

46 + 39 = ☐

b 60 + 30 = ☐

63 + 30 = ☐

63 + 29 = ☐

c 50 + 50 = ☐

54 + 50 = ☐

54 + 49 = ☐

d 70 + 40 = ☐

75 + 40 = ☐

75 + 39 = ☐

e 80 + 30 = ☐

86 + 30 = ☐

86 + 29 = ☐

f 90 + 50 = ☐

94 + 50 = ☐

94 + 49 = ☐

2 Draw lines to join pairs that total 100.

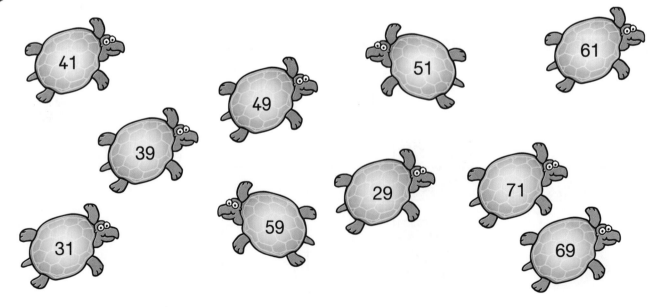

41   49   51   61

39   29   71

31   59   69

Equivalent fractions

Some fractions are **equivalent**.

This means they look different, but are worth the same value.

These are all equivalent to $\frac{1}{2}$.

$\frac{2}{4}$ $\frac{3}{6}$ $\frac{4}{8}$ $\frac{5}{10}$

1 Put a cross through the odd one out.

a

b
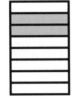

c

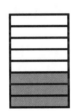 

2 Write each fraction in two ways. The first one has been done for you.

a

$\frac{2}{6}$ and $\frac{1}{3}$

c
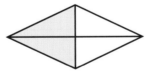

$\frac{\Box}{\Box}$ and $\frac{\Box}{\Box}$

e

$\frac{\Box}{\Box}$ and $\frac{\Box}{\Box}$

b
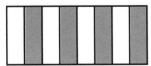

$\frac{\Box}{\Box}$ and $\frac{\Box}{\Box}$

d

$\frac{\Box}{\Box}$ and $\frac{\Box}{\Box}$

f
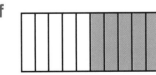

$\frac{\Box}{\Box}$ and $\frac{\Box}{\Box}$

23

Adding and subtracting fractions

Like fractions are fractions with the same **denominator** (bottom number). You can add and subtract like fractions easily. Simply add or subtract the **numerators** (top numbers) and then write answer over the **common denominator**.

Find $\dfrac{1}{5} + \dfrac{2}{5}$

$\dfrac{1}{5} + \dfrac{2}{5} = \dfrac{3}{5}$

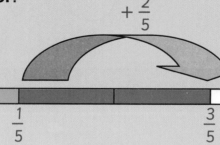

$+\dfrac{2}{5}$

$\dfrac{1}{5}$ $\dfrac{3}{5}$ $-\dfrac{3}{8}$

Find $\dfrac{7}{8} - \dfrac{3}{8}$

$\dfrac{7}{8} - \dfrac{3}{8} = \dfrac{4}{8} = \dfrac{1}{2}$

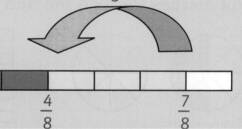

$\dfrac{4}{8}$ $\dfrac{7}{8}$

---

1 Answer these fraction calculations giving the answer in the simplest form. Use the bars to help you.

a $\dfrac{5}{7} + \dfrac{2}{7} = \boxed{}$

b $\dfrac{2}{6} + \dfrac{1}{6} = \boxed{}$

c $\dfrac{1}{4} + \dfrac{2}{4} = \boxed{}$

d $\dfrac{4}{15} + \dfrac{6}{15} = \boxed{}$

e $\dfrac{1}{9} + \dfrac{4}{9} = \boxed{}$

f $\dfrac{13}{14} - \dfrac{1}{14} = \boxed{}$

g $\dfrac{5}{8} - \dfrac{2}{8} = \boxed{}$

h $\dfrac{3}{7} - \dfrac{2}{7} = \boxed{}$

i $\dfrac{9}{18} - \dfrac{3}{18} = \boxed{}$

j $\dfrac{9}{12} - \dfrac{3}{12} = \boxed{}$

Mental subtraction

What is 54 − 28?

A good way of working this out in your head is to **count on**.

28 on to 30 is 2
30 on to 54 is 24
24 add 2 is 26
so 54 − 28 = 26

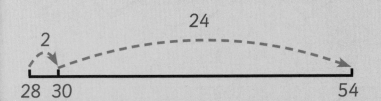

1 Answer these questions.

a 40 − 28 =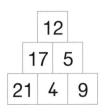

e 46 − 28 =

i 55 − 29 =

b 70 − 39 =

f 44 − 19 =

j 64 − 39 =

c 90 − 47 =

g 53 − 27 =

k 56 − 37 =

d 38 − 29 =

h 61 − 38 =

l 62 − 47 =

2 The difference between two numbers that are next to each other is written in the box above them. Write the missing numbers.

```
      12
    17   5
  21   4   9
```

a
```
  26  12  18
```

b
```
      3
     14
    7   18
```

c
```
   21  13
      6
```

d
```
     9
       6
     3
```

Money problems

You often need to work out how much **change** is needed.

To calculate change, count on from the price of the item to the amount of money given.

£1 and 40p → 10p → £1 and 50p → 50p → £2

The change from £2 is 60p.

---

1 Write the answers to these money problems.

a Work out the change from £1.

b Work out the change from £2.

c Work out the change from £5.

75p change: ☐ p

 £1 and 60p change: ☐ p

 £3 and 50p change: £ ☐

68p change: ☐ p

 £1 and 25p change: ☐ p

 £2 and 80p change: £ ☐

89p change: ☐ p

 £1 and 85p change: ☐ p

 £1 and 90p change: £ ☐

---

2 Answer the money problems.

a Leon buys 2 books. They cost £2 and £2 and 20p. How much change will he receive from £5?

☐

b Alexis bought a CD. She had 20p change from a £10 note. How much was her CD?

☐

c Which 2 items when bought together will cost £5?

_____

d What will be the total cost of all 3 items?

☐

26

Right angles

A right angle is a **quarter of a turn**.

A **complete turn** is the same as **four right angles**.

Here are four compass directions.

You can turn **clockwise**

or **anticlockwise**

---

1 Tick each right angle.

a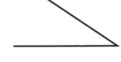

b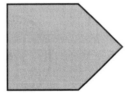

---

2 Write the direction you will face after turning.

a Start facing north. Turn 1 right angle anticlockwise.

_____

b Start facing east. Turn 1 right angle clockwise.

_____

c Start facing west. Turn 2 right angles clockwise.

_____

d Start facing south. Turn 3 right angles anticlockwise.

_____

Time

On a clock face, read the **minutes past the hour** to tell the time.

As the minute hand moves around the clock, the hour hand moves towards the next hour.

5:42

42 minutes past 5
or 18 minutes to 6

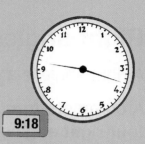

9:18

18 minutes past 9

1 Write the times shown on each clock.

a 　　b 　　c 　　d

_____　　_____　　_____　　_____

Draw the hands on these clocks.

e 　　f 　　g 　　h

　　7.56　　　　　　9.03　　　　　　3.41　　　　　　11.18

2 Write the number of minutes between each of these times.

a

 minutes

c

[ ] minutes

b

[ ] minutes

d

[ ] minutes

28

Handling data

Some graphs use **bars** or **columns** to show information.

Pictograms use pictures to show information.

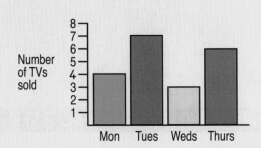

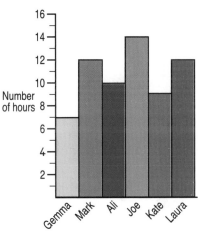

1 This graph shows the number of hours a group of children watch television in a week.

a Who watched television the most? _____

b How many hours did Gemma watch? _____

c How many more hours of television did Laura watch than Kate? _____

d How many fewer hours did Ali watch than Joe? _____

e Which two children watched the same amount of television?

_____ and _____

2 Carry out a TV watching survey.

- Ask family or friends to work out how many hours of TV they watch in a week.

- Record your results as a pictogram.

☐ = 2 hours.

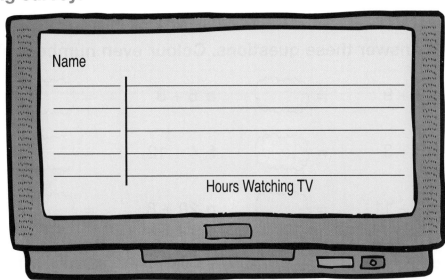

Odd and even numbers

Odd numbers always end in

1 3 5 7 9

Even numbers always end in

0 2 4 6 8

Look at the ones digit of a number:

14**5** is odd 15**4** is even

1 Colour all the odd numbers red.

74	46	108	94	114	136	28	150	96
102	85	77	109	192	59	261	395	128
314	61	100	205	116	299	94	105	306
108	93	209	183	318	417	89	101	200
52	74	82	211	260	300	192	245	412
112	196	418	309	234	108	386	193	350
376	190	210	106	92	34	76	84	272

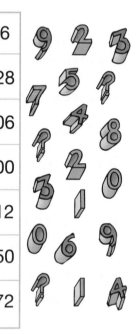

What odd number do the red squares create?

2 Answer these questions. Colour even numbers blue and odd numbers red.

a 7 + 9 =

b 5 + 3 =

c 9 + 11 =

d odd + odd =

e 6 + 8 =

f 4 + 12 =

g 20 + 8 =

h even + even =

i 7 + 4 =

j 9 + 10 =

k 15 + 2 =

l odd + even =

Numbers to 1000

3-digit numbers are made from **hundreds, tens** and **ones**.

hundreds   tens   ones

460 → 400 + 60

1 Complete this table. The first row has been done for you.

143	100 + 40 + 3	one hundred and forty-three	hundreds tens ones
251			hundreds tens ones
	700 + 30 + 6		hundreds tens ones
			hundreds tens ones
		nine hundred and seventy-six	hundreds tens ones

2 Use the digits 3 4 6.

a How many different 3-digit numbers can you make? _____

b Write them in order, starting with the smallest.

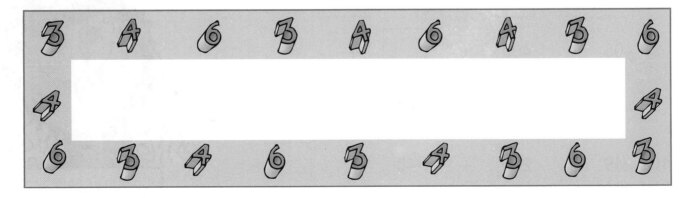

Test 1 Place value

There are **10 digits** which are **0, 1, 2, 3, 4, 5, 6, 7, 8** and **9**.
Digits are used to build up larger numbers.
The position of a digit in a number changes its value.

hundreds	tens	ones	
6	3	1	= 600 + 30 + 1
3	1	4	= 300 + 10 + 4

Write the numbers to match the words.

1. sixty ⇨ ☐

2. six hundred and sixty ⇨ ☐

3. six hundred and six ⇨ ☐

4. sixteen ⇨ ☐

5. six hundred and sixty-six ⇨ ☐

Write the missing numbers.

6. 633 = 600 + 30 + ☐

7. 910 = ☐ + 10 + 0

8. 405 = 400 + ☐ + 5

9. 468 = ☐ + 60 + 8

10. 249 = 200 + 40 + ☐

Colour in your score

Test 2 Addition and subtraction

Knowing **number facts** can help you
to work out other calculations.

$7 + 6 = 13$

$70 + 60 = 130$

$700 + 600 = 1300$

$12 - 6 = 6$

$120 - 60 = 60$

$1200 - 600 = 600$

Answer these.

1. $40 + 70 =$

2. $90 - 30 =$

3. $130 - 50 =$

4. $600 + 800 =$

5. $900 - 400 =$

6. $1200 + 500 =$

7. $900 + 700 =$

8. $170 - 80 =$

9. $190 - 120 =$

10. $800 + 500 =$

Colour in your score

33

Test 3 Word problems: addition and subtraction

Learn these **addition** words:

altogether TOTAL sum
add
more than
greater than plus

Learn these **subtraction** words:

less than take away
minus subtract LEAVES
fewer than difference

Answer these questions.

1. Which number is 173 minus 5?

2. What is the sum of 234 and 40?

3. What is 572 take away 200?

4. What number is 30 less than 272?

5. What is 432 add 500?

6. Tom goes shopping with £2. He spends 80p. How much does he have left?

7. Nigel has 75 points and Alison has 35. How many more points has Nigel?

8. Peta has 16 sweets. She eats 4 and gives 8 to Jan. How many sweets does she have left?

9. Ellen and Joe spend 87p each. How much do they spend altogether?

10. Rebecca has £2 and 75p. Her friend gives her 15p. How much money does Rebecca have now?

10
9
8
7
6
5
4
3
2
1

Colour in your score

Test 4 2-D shapes

Name	Number of sides
triangle	3
quadrilateral	4
pentagon	5
hexagon	6
heptagon	7
octagon	8

Write the name of each shape.

1. _____

2. _____

3. _____

4. _____

5. _____

Draw one line of symmetry on each shape.

6.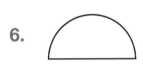

7.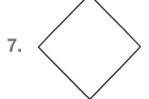

8.

9.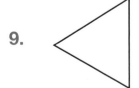

10.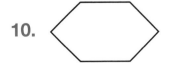

Colour in your score

Test 5 Numbers: counting and properties

When you add a small number to a larger number, you can **count on**. It is easier to count on from the larger number.

134 + 3 is easier to count than 3 + 134.

Add 4 to each number.

1.  89 [ ]

2.  148 [ ]

3.  707 [ ]

4.  666 [ ]

5.  415 [ ]

Write the answers.

6. 40 + 912 = [ ]

7. 396 + 5 = [ ]

8. 700 + 108 = [ ]

9. 909 + 100 = [ ]

10. 70 + 644 = [ ]

10
9
8
7
6
5
4
3
2
1

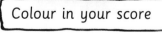
Colour in your score

36

Test 6 Multiplication tables

When you **multiply numbers** the order does not matter.
Look at both numbers and choose which way you prefer.

5 × 7 has the **same answer** as 7 × 5.

2 × 8 has the **same answer** as 8 × 2.

Answer these.

1. | 8 | × 5 ➡ | |

2. | 9 | × 2 ➡ | |

3. | 6 | × 10 ➡ | |

4. | 7 | × 5 ➡ | |

5. | 4 | × 2 ➡ | |

6. | 11 | × 3 ➡ | |

7. | 5 | × 8 ➡ | |

8. | 2 | × 7 ➡ | |

9. | 5 | × 9 ➡ | |

10. | 12 | × 4 ➡ | |

Colour in your score

Test 7 Money (1)

Working out **change** need not be too difficult.
You must be able to make amounts up to **£1**.

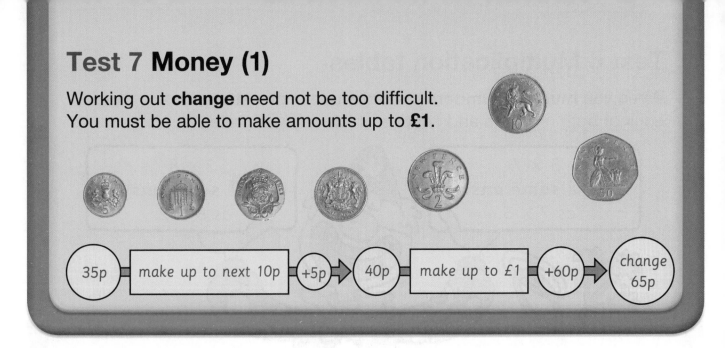

35p — make up to next 10p — +5p → 40p — make up to £1 — +60p → change 65p

Write the total amount of money in each piggybank.

The money in each purse is given to pay the price shown on each label. Write the change.

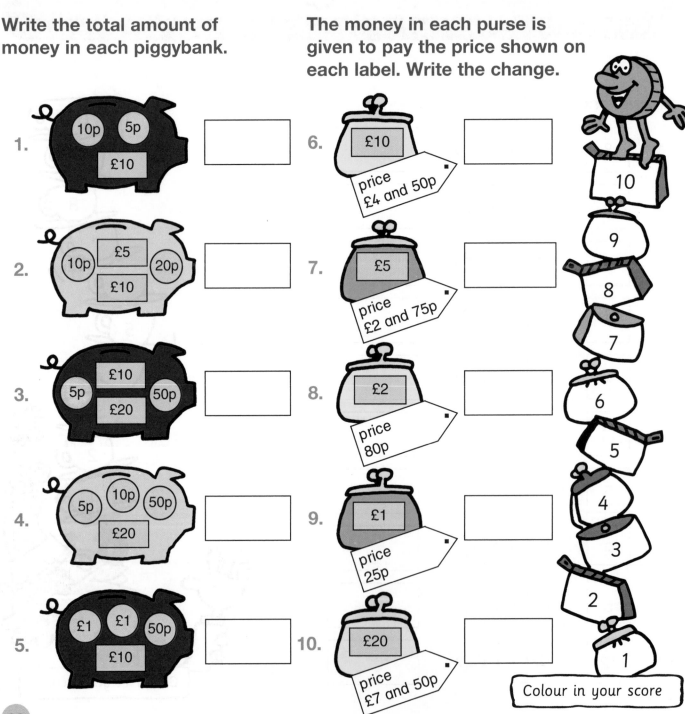

1. 10p 5p £10 [ ]

2. £5 10p 20p £10 [ ]

3. £10 5p 50p £20 [ ]

4. 5p 10p 50p £20 [ ]

5. £1 £1 50p £10 [ ]

6. £10 price £4 and 50p [ ]

7. £5 price £2 and 75p [ ]

8. £2 price 80p [ ]

9. £1 price 25p [ ]

10. £20 price £7 and 50p [ ]

10
9
8
7
6
5
4
3
2
1

Colour in your score

38

Test 8 Fractions (1)

Some **fractions** are **equivalent**. This means they are worth the same.

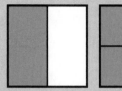

$$\frac{1}{2} = \frac{2}{4}$$

$$\frac{1}{4} = \frac{2}{8}$$

$$\frac{1}{3} = \frac{2}{6}$$

Write each fraction in two ways.

1. _____ and _____

2. _____ and _____

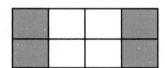

3. _____ and _____

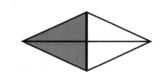

4. _____ and _____

5. _____ and _____

Colour these fractions.

6. $\frac{2}{3}$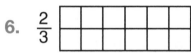

7. $\frac{1}{5}$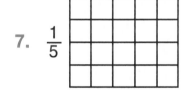

8. $\frac{7}{10}$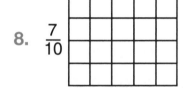

9. $\frac{3}{4}$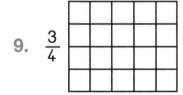

10. $\frac{1}{6}$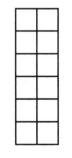

10
9
8
7
6
5
4
3
2
1

Colour in your score

Test 9 Time (1)

It is sometimes important to work out **the difference between two times**. Time is a way of measuring how long something lasts, or how long before things start or come to an end.

To find the difference between two times use a number line.

The first lesson began at 8:10 and ended at 9:20. How long was the lesson?

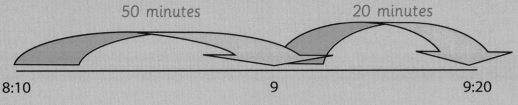

50 minutes   20 minutes

8:10   9   9:20

50 minutes + 20 minutes = 70 minutes = 1 hour 10 minutes

Read this information and then answer the questions below.

Baker Pat arrived at the bakery at 6.50.
He started to bake some cookies at 7.05.
The cookies were put in the oven at 7.35.
The cookies were ready at 8.05 and then left to cool for 15 minutes.
Icing the cookies finished at 8:40.
Baker Pat immediately started putting the cookies on a tray and had them all on at 8.55, and tidied up!
The bakery opened at 9:00 and closed at midday.

1. How long did the cookies take to bake in the oven? _____

2. How long did it take the baker to ice the cookies? _____

3. How long did it take the baker to place the cookies on the tray?

   _____

4. How many minutes did the baker have to tidy up before the

   bakery opened? _____

5. How long was the bakery open for? _____

Draw the hands on each clock to show the time.

6. | 8.55 | 7. | 3.45 | 8. | 10.35 | 9. | 12.40 | 10. | 1.05 |

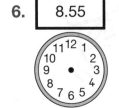

Colour in your score

Test 10 Data handling

In a Venn diagram the area **outside** the circles is also important.

Things which are coloured **and** triangles go in the overlap.

Things which are not coloured **and** not triangles go outside the circles.

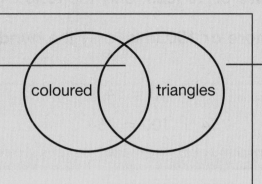

Draw each shape on this diagram.

1.
2.
3.
4.
5.

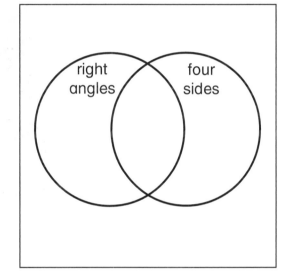

Draw each shape on this diagram.

6.
7.
8.
9.
10.

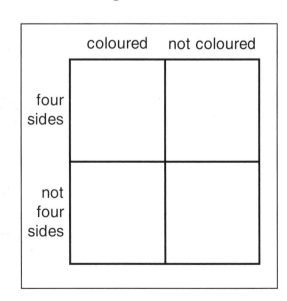

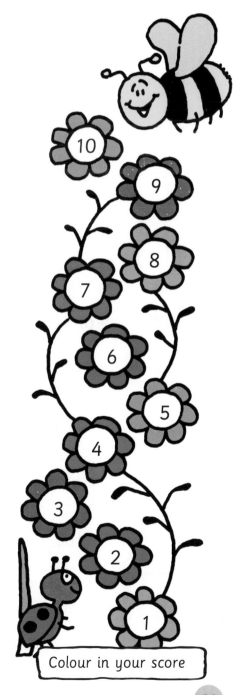

Colour in your score

Test 11 Finding 10 or 100 more or less

When we find **10 more or 10 less**, only the **tens** digit changes.

When we find **100 more or 100 less**, only the **hundreds** digit changes.

$$74 - 10 = 64$$
$$764 + 100 = 864$$

Find 10 more or 10 less.

1. $64 + 10 =$ ☐

2. $98 - 10 =$ ☐

3. $34 - $ ☐ $= 24$

4. $89 + $ ☐ $= 99$

5. $88 - $ ☐ $= 78$

Find 100 more or 100 less.

6. $634 + 100 =$ ☐

7. $952 - 100 =$ ☐

8. $170 + $ ☐ $= 270$

9. ☐ $+ 100 = 736$

10. ☐ $- 100 = 53$

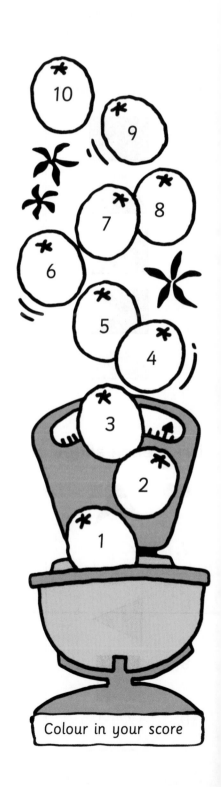

Colour in your score

Test 12 Addition

Here is a useful method when adding larger numbers.

When numbers get too large to use mental calculation strategies, you need another method. You can use a method known as a **formal written method** by setting out the calculations on paper and making sure you line the numbers in the correct place value columns (hundreds, tens and units).

$$
\begin{array}{r}
\text{HTU} \\
559 \\
+\ 262 \\
\hline
821 \\
\hline
{\scriptstyle 1\ 1}
\end{array}
$$

Do these on paper.

1. 314 + 62 =

2. 158 + 21 =

3. 828 + 33 =

4. 569 + 54 =

5. 729 + 59 =

6. 745 + 254 =

7. 554 + 369 =

8. 423 + 567 =

9. 653 + 378 =

10. 137 + 642 =

10
9
8
7
6
5
4
3
2
1

Colour in your score

Test 13 Word problems: multiplication and division

Learn these **multiplication** words:

multiply TIMES **lots of** product multiplication multiple

Learn these **division** words:

factor **remainder** **halve** SHARE divide division quotient

Answer these questions.

1. What is the quotient of 20 and 5?

2. What is 2 multiplied by 9?

3. What is 60 shared by 10?

4. What is 10 times 8?

5. What is 20 divided by 2?

6. Liz has 10 pencils. Amy has half as many. How many pencils has Amy?

7. Arlo buys 8 tokens costing 5p each. How much money does he need?

8. Kim has 50p. How many 5p sweets can she buy?

9. Phil puts 8 stamps on each page. He has to fill 5 pages. How many stamps would he need?

10. Marco has 60p to share between his 6 friends. How much will each friend get?

Colour in your score

Test 14 3-D shapes

If you slice a **prism** into equal lengths all the slices are the **same shape and size**.

triangular prism	hexagonal prism	not a prism
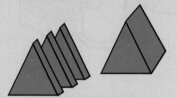		
All the slices will be the same.	All the slices will be the same.	All the slices will be different sizes.

Draw a line from each shape to where it goes on the diagram.

	prism	not a prism

1.

2.

3.

4.

5.

6.

7.

8.

9.

10.

Colour in your score

9 10

8 7

4 5 6

3 2 1

45

Test 15 Measures and time

You need to remember **equivalent** measurements.

1 m	=	100 cm	1 l	=	1000 ml	1 hour	= 60 minutes
1 cm	=	10 mm	1 kg	=	1000 g	1 minute	= 60 seconds
			1 km	=	1000 m		

Answer these questions.

1. $\frac{3}{4}$ metre $=$ ☐ cm

2. 2 kilograms $=$ ☐ g

3. 2 kilometres $=$ ☐ m

4. $\frac{1}{2}$ litre $=$ ☐ ml

5. 2 cm $=$ ☐ mm

6. $\frac{1}{2}$ hour $=$ ☐ minutes

7. $\frac{3}{4}$ hour $=$ ☐ minutes

8. $\frac{1}{4}$ hour $=$ ☐ minutes

9. $\frac{1}{2}$ minute $=$ ☐ seconds

10. $\frac{3}{4}$ minute $=$ ☐ seconds

Colour in your score

Test 16 Number patterns

The **last digit** of a number will tell you whether it is odd or even.

If the ending is
1   3   5   7 or **9**
the number is

odd

If the ending is
0   2   4   6 or **8**
the number is

even

Continue these number patterns.

1. [601] [611] [621] ⬡ ⬡ ⬡

2. [789] [689] [589] ⬡ ⬡ ⬡

3. [28] [38] [48] ⬡ ⬡ ⬡

4. [99] [89] [79] ⬡ ⬡ ⬡

5. [355] [455] [555] ⬡ ⬡ ⬡

Write each number correctly on the diagram.

	odd	not odd
6. 39		
7. 345		
8. 216		
9. 572		
10. 481		

Colour in your score

47

Test 17 Multiplication and division

Multiplying by 2 and doubling are the same.

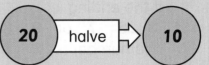

10) double ⟹ 20

Dividing by 2 and halving are the same.

20) halve ⟹ 10

Doubling and halving are opposites.

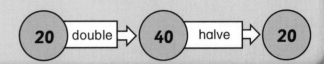

20) double ⟹ 40) halve ⟹ 20

Double each of these.

1. 150 double ⟹ [ ]

2. £75 double ⟹ [ ]

3. 80 cm double ⟹ [ ]

4. 120 m double ⟹ [ ]

5. 15p double ⟹ [ ]

Halve each of these.

6. 90 halve ⟹ [ ]

7. £24 halve ⟹ [ ]

8. 66 cm halve ⟹ [ ]

9. 24 kg halve ⟹ [ ]

10. 50p halve ⟹ [ ]

Colour in your score

48

Test 18 Money (2)

When writing **money totals**, always put the pounds together and the pence separately, like this:

£1 + 20p + 20p + £2 +

10p = £3 and 50p

Remember 100p = £1 so 205p = £2 and 5p

Total these.

1. 20p ▸ 50p ▸ £1 ▸ [ ]

2. £1 ▸ 5p ▸ £1 ▸ [ ]

3. £2 ▸ £1 ▸ 10p ▸ [ ]

4. 50p ▸ 50p ▸ 1p ▸ [ ]

5. 2p ▸ 5p ▸ £2 ▸ [ ]

Write how many pennies are in these amounts.

6. £7 and 54p [ ]

7. £2 and 7p [ ]

8. £3 and 49p [ ]

9. £9 and 12p [ ]

10. £1 and 77p [ ]

Colour in your score

49

Test 19 Fractions (2)

$\frac{1}{3}$ of 15 **is the same as** 15 ÷ 3 = 5

Work out the answers.

1. $\frac{1}{4}$ of 12 =

2. $\frac{1}{2}$ of 28 =

3. $\frac{1}{3}$ of 18 =

4. $\frac{1}{5}$ of 20 =

5. $\frac{1}{4}$ of 16 =

6. $\frac{1}{10}$ of 60 =

7. $\frac{2}{3}$ of 24 =

8. $\frac{2}{5}$ of 35 =

9. $\frac{3}{4}$ of 32 =

10. $\frac{3}{10}$ of 90 =

Colour in your score

Test 20 Data (1)

We often write information in **lists** and **tables**.

The **order** and **position** of the information is important.

The order of lists can be things like: **alphabetical**, **size**, **date order**.

Tables have **columns** going down and **rows** going across.

Where people live				
	Road	Street	Avenue	Lane
Morris	✓			
Jenny		✓		
Ravi				✓
Sol			✓	

Use the table above to answer these questions.

1. Who lives in a street? _____

2. Who lives in a lane? _____

3. Where does Morris live? _____

4. Where does Sol live? _____

5. Where does Ravi live? _____

Write the following lists in the columns below.

6. Peter, George and Lucy in alphabetical order.

7. April, February and November in date order.

8. 635g, 480g and 755g in order, starting with the lightest.

9. Lee, Sandra and Eric by word length, starting with the least number of letters.

10. 35 seconds, 1 minute and $\frac{1}{2}$ minute in order, starting with the shortest time.

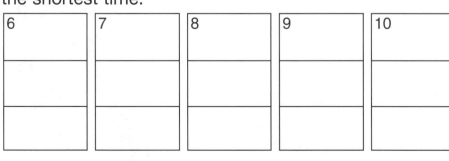

6	7	8	9	10

Colour in your score

Test 21 Telling the time with 12- and 24-hour clocks

When you write the time using the 12-hour digital clock you must always write **am** or **pm**. This is because the hands of a 12-hour clock go round twice in one day and you need to show which part of the day you mean.

The 24-hour clock uses numbers from 0 to 24 to stand for all the hours in the day. Always use four digits to write the time of the 24-hour clock.

00:00 (or 24:00) is midnight. After midday the hours become 13, 14, 15, etc (e.g. 6 pm is shown as 18:00).

For each clock face, write the time using the 12-hour digital clock.

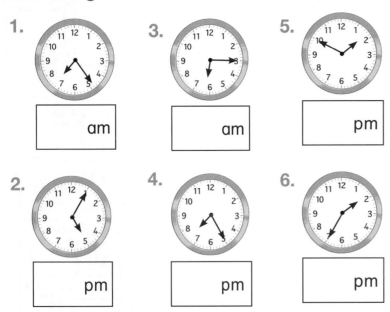

1.
```
am
```

3.
```
am
```

5.
```
pm
```

2.
```
pm
```

4.
```
pm
```

6.
```
pm
```

Match the 12-hour digital clock times to the correct 24-hour digital clock times.

12-hour digital clock	24-hour digital clock
7. 1.30 pm	09:45
8. 9.45 am	13:30
9. 6.15 pm	19:20
10. 7.20 pm	18:15

10

9

8

7

6

5

4

3

2

1

Colour in your score

52

Test 22 Subtraction

Here is a useful method for **subtracting** larger numbers.

When numbers get too large to use mental calculation strategies, you need to use a **formal written method**. Set out the calculations on paper and making sure you line up the numbers in the correct place value columns (hundreds, tens and units).

```
H T U
5⁴¹3
-1 4 2
  3 7 1
```

Answer these using a formal written method.

1. 946 − 41 =

2. 595 − 64 =

3. 397 − 71 =

4. 671 − 79 =

5. 285 − 67 =

6. 691 − 327 =

7. 322 − 254 =

8. 573 − 494 =

9. 792 − 473 =

10. 573 − 166 =

Colour in your score

Test 23 **Money problems**

When adding several amounts, it sometimes helps to make a list, then total.

Remember 100p = £1

19p   40p   25p   54p   30p   48p   15p   24p

lolly	19p
ice-cream	25p
pizza	54p
total	98p

What is the total cost of the following?

1. 1 lolly, 1 hot dog, 1 ice-cream cone and 1 slice of pizza

2. 2 hot dogs and 2 slices of pizza

3. 1 ice-cream cone and 2 lollies

4. 1 ice-cream cone, 2 slices of pizza and 1 hot dog

5. 1 slice of pizza and 2 lollies

How much change from £1 would you have if you bought the following?

6. 3 bowls of ice-cream

7. 1 milkshake and 1 slice of pie

8. 1 slice of pie and 1 hamburger

9. 2 hamburgers

10. 1 bowl of ice-cream and 2 milkshakes

Colour in your score

Test 24 Shapes: right angles

A **right angle** is a $\frac{1}{4}$ of a whole turn.

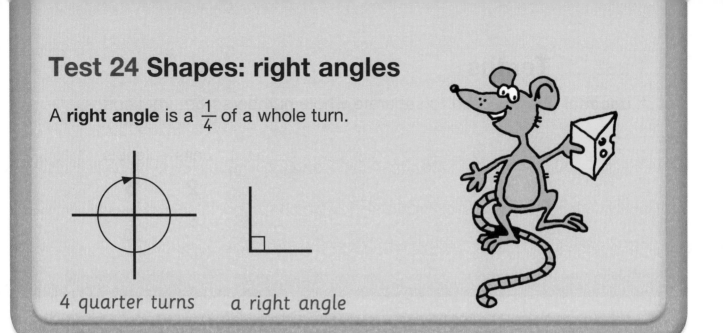

4 quarter turns   a right angle

Circle the right angles in the shapes below.

Tick the right angles and cross the angles that are not right angles.

1.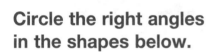

2.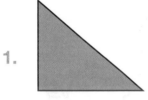

3.

4.

5.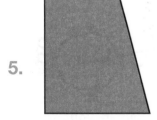

6. 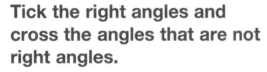 ☐

7. ☐

8.  ☐

9.  ☐

10.  ☐

Colour in your score

Test 25 **Tenths**

A **decimal point** is used to separate whole numbers from fractions.

$0 . 1 = \frac{1}{10}$ $0 . 2 = \frac{2}{10}$ $0 . 5 = \frac{1}{2}$

units	tenths
2	**· 6**
2	$\frac{6}{10}$

Change these fractions to decimals.

1. $\frac{7}{10}$ = ☐

2. $1\frac{1}{2}$ = ☐

3. $3\frac{3}{10}$ = ☐

4. $\frac{9}{10}$ = ☐

5. $2\frac{4}{10}$ = ☐

Write the decimals on this number line.

6. ☐ 7. ☐ 8. ☐ 9. ☐ 10. ☐

0 ├─┼─┼─┼─┼─┼─┼─┼─┼─┼─┤ 1

Colour in your score

Test 26 **Division**

Use multiplication to help work out **division** questions.

$$24 \div 6 = \boxed{} \Rightarrow 6 \times \boxed{} = 24$$
$$6 \times 4 = 24$$
$$\Downarrow$$
$$24 \div 6 = 4$$

If a number cannot be divided exactly, it leaves a remainder.

$$26 \div 4 = 6 \text{ remainder } 2$$

Answer these.

1. $30 \div 5 = \boxed{}$

2. $32 \div 4 = \boxed{}$

3. $42 \div 3 = \boxed{}$

4. $52 \div 2 = \boxed{}$

5. $85 \div 5 = \boxed{}$

Answer these and write the remainder.

6. $34 \div 4 = \boxed{}$ remainder $\boxed{}$

7. $29 \div 2 = \boxed{}$ remainder $\boxed{}$

8. $58 \div 5 = \boxed{}$ remainder $\boxed{}$

9. $47 \div 3 = \boxed{}$ remainder $\boxed{}$

10. $86 \div 10 = \boxed{}$ remainder $\boxed{}$

Colour in your score

Test 27 Problems

- When answering **word problems** you must read the words **carefully**.

- Decide whether it is an **add**, **subtract**, **multiply** or **divide** problem.

- Look at your answer and ask yourself if it seems a sensible answer to the problem.

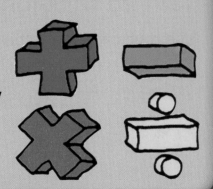

What time will it be half an hour after the times shown on these 12-hour clocks?

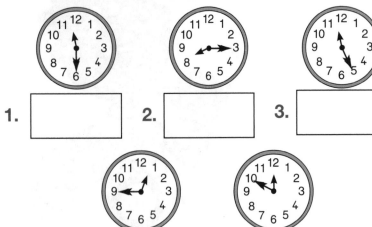

1. [ ]   2. [ ]   3. [ ]

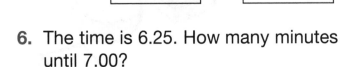

4. [ ]   5. [ ]

6. The time is 6.25. How many minutes until 7.00?

7. The paper bill comes to £2 and 2p. How much change will there be from £5?

8. If 6 bread rolls cost £3 and 36p, how much does 1 roll cost?

9. Rebecca is 1 hour late for her swimming lesson. It is now 3.30 pm. What time should she have been there?

10. Carly had 35 conkers in each of her 2 pockets. How many conkers did she have altogether?

Colour in your score

Test 28 Multiplication

When **multiplying** it can help to break numbers up.

$$43 \times 5 = \quad 40 \times 5 = \quad 200$$
$$3 \times 5 = \quad + \underline{15}$$
$$43 \times 5 = \quad 215$$

$$\begin{array}{r} 4\,3 \\ \times \quad 5 \\ \hline 2\,1\,5 \\ {\scriptstyle 1} \end{array}$$

Answer these.

1. 36 × 3 =

2. 41 × 4 =

3. 53 × 2 =

4. 47 × 3 =

5. 56 × 4 =

Answer these.

6. $\begin{array}{r} 5\,3 \\ \times \quad 3 \\ \hline \end{array}$

7. $\begin{array}{r} 8\,4 \\ \times \quad 2 \\ \hline \end{array}$

8. $\begin{array}{r} 6\,7 \\ \times \quad 4 \\ \hline \end{array}$

9. $\begin{array}{r} 7\,4 \\ \times \quad 3 \\ \hline \end{array}$

10. $\begin{array}{r} 5\,9 \\ \times \quad 5 \\ \hline \end{array}$

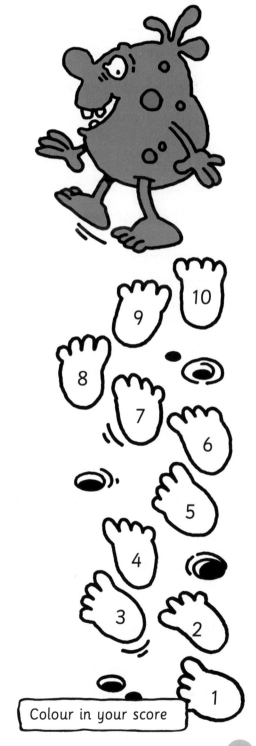

Colour in your score

59

Test 29 Time (2)

Calendars show us **months** and **days of the month**.

December						
Su	**Mo**	**Tu**	**We**	**Th**	**Fr**	**Sa**
				1	2	3
4	5	6	7	8	9	10
11	12	13	14	15	16	17
18	19	20	21	22	23	24
25	26	27	28	29	30	31

Use the calendar above to help you answer these.

1. What day of the week is the first day of December?

   _____

2. What day of the week was the last day of November?

   _____

3. What day of the week will the first day of January be?

   _____

4. How many Fridays are there in December?

   _____

5. How many Saturdays and Sundays are there altogether in December?

   _____

6. What date is 3 weeks after the 5th December?

   _____

7. What day of the week is the 25th December?

   _____

8. What date is 2 weeks before the 16th December?

   _____

9. What month is December in the year?

   _____

10. What month follows December?

    _____

Colour in your score

Test 30 **Data (2)**

On **picture graphs** the picture does not always show 1 of something.

It sometimes shows quantities such as **2, 5, 10** or **100**.

You have to look for the **key** to help you.

Key: **1 ball = 5 people**

Favourite ball games	
football	⚽⚽⚽⚽⚽
rugby	🏈🏈🏈
table tennis	○○
tennis	🎾🎾🎾🎾
basketball	🏀

Children were asked about their favourite ball games.

1. How many children chose football?

2. How many children chose basketball?

3. How many children chose tennis?

4. How many children chose table tennis or rugby?

5. How many children chose tennis or football?

6. How many more children chose football than rugby?

7. How many more children chose tennis than table tennis?

8. Which game was most popular? _____

9. Which game was least popular? _____

10. How many children altogether were asked about their favourite ball game?

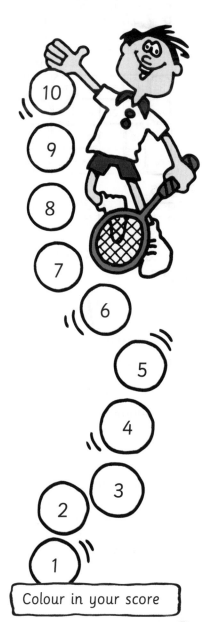

Colour in your score

61

ANSWERS

Page 2
a 33, 36, 39
b 36, 42, 48
c 36, 40, 44
d 60, 50, 40
e 55, 50, 45
f 104, 106, 108

2. a 78, 84, 90, 96
b 120, 130, 140, 150
c 24, 32, 40, 48, 56

Page 3
1. a 80   **f** 300, 4
b 5   **g** 600 + 20 + 7
c 100, 3   **h** 800 + 10 + 3
d 10, 6   **i** 900 + 40 + 5
e 500, 50   **j** 700 + 90 + 9

2. a 350   **b** 470   **c** 704

Page 4
1. a 12, 120, 1200   **g** 120
b 15, 150, 1500   **h** 1300
c 15, 150, 1500   **i** 1300
d 7, 70, 700   **j** 1800
e 8, 80, 800   **k** 240
f 9, 90, 900   **l** 40
                      m 1600

2.

34	51	59	41	76	82	38	62
66	75	25	65	24	47	53	77
91	19	72	83	17	45	96	13
24	81	74	56	35	55	48	52

Page 5
1. a 36   **c** 36   **e** 76
b 35   **d** 38   **f** 69

2. a 26 kg   **c** 60 kg   **e** 76 kg
b 28 kg   **d** 46 kg   **f** 77 kg

Page 6
1. a

triangles

b

pentagons

c

quadrilaterals

d

hexagons

2.

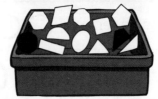

Page 7
1. a 87 cm, 107 cm, 137 cm, 170 cm, 207 cm
b 225 ml, 272 ml, 275 ml, 308 ml, 340 ml
c £1 and 9p, £1 and 38p, £1 and 70p, £1 and 95p, £2 and 5p
d 525 m, 608 m, 610 m, 635 m, 802 m

2. a 19 and 16
b 48 and 42
c 63 and 36
d 215 and 206

Page 8
1. a May
b Saturday
c 14th
d 26th
e Friday
f Wednesday

Page 9
1. a
 **c**

b   **d**

2. a 9   **d** 10   **g** 15
b 2   **e** 24   **h** 14
c 12   **f** 2

Page 10
1. a $4\frac{1}{2}$ cm   **d** 7 cm
b $8\frac{1}{2}$ cm   **e** $3\frac{1}{2}$ cm
c $6\frac{1}{2}$ cm   **f** 9 cm

2. Check your child's lines with a ruler.

Page 11
1. a 20, 70, 80, 100, 30, 90
b 10, 35, 40, 30, 15, 45
c 4, 14, 16, 12, 6, 18
d 48, 28, 32, 44, 36, 64
e 48, 56, 55, 12, 24, 96

2. a D U N D E E
b E D I N B U R G H

Page 12
1. a 94   **g** 131
b 101   **h** 141
c 64   **i** 171
d 148   **j** 256
e 165   **k** 251
f 126   **l** 301

2. a 444   **d** 1001
b 355   **e** 754
c 620   **f** 810

Page 13
1. a
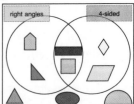

b
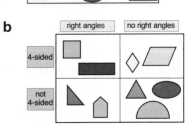

2. a D **b** C **c** A **d** B **e** A

Page 14
1. a 4 kg   **c** 9 kg   **e** 8 kg
b 7 kg   **d** 10 kg   **f** 13 kg

2. a 10   **c** 5   **e** 10
b 2   **d** 4

Page 15
1. a 50p, 20p, 10p coins
b £1, 10p, 5p coins
c £2, 50p, 5p coins
d £2, £1, 10p coins
e £1, 20p, 20p, 5p coins
f £1, 50p, 20p, 10p coins
g £2, 20p, 10p, 5p coins
h £2, £2, 50p, 5p coins

2. a Total 70p
50p, 10p, 10p coins
b Total £1 and 80p
£1, 50p, 20p, 10p coins

Page 16
1. a 14 cm   **c** 10 cm
b 14 cm   **d** 12 cm

2. a 16 cm   **d** 20 cm
b 14 cm   **e** 14 cm
c 20 cm

Page 17
1. a 80   **d** 41   **g** 270
b 16   **e** 13   **h** 350
c 40   **f** 25

2. a 50p, 15p, 35p or 40p, 35p, 25p
b 70p, 30p, 40p, 10p

Page 18

1.
a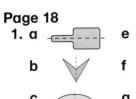
e

b

f

c

g

d

h

2. a  b

Page 19

1. a 60ml   c 90ml   e 800ml
   b 20ml   d 500ml   f 400ml

2. a 1000ml   d 100ml
   b 500ml   e 5
   c 250ml   f 10

Page 20

1. a 6 remainder 1
   b 4 remainder 2
   c 5 remainder 2
   d 3 remainder 3
   e 3 remainder 1
   f 6 remainder 2

2.

Page 21

1. a 5 faces, pyramid
   b 6 faces, cube
   c 5 faces, prism
   d 4 faces, pyramid
   e 6 faces, cuboid
   f 7 faces, prism

2.

	prism	not a prism
1 or more triangle faces	a c	b f
no triangle faces	d e	g

Page 22

1. a 80, 86, 85
   b 90, 93, 92
   c 100, 104, 103
   d 110, 115, 114
   e 110, 116, 115
   f 140, 144, 143

2. 51 → 49   41 → 59
   61 → 39   29 → 71
   69 → 31

Page 23

1. a 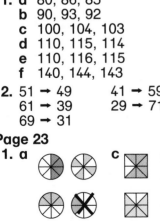   c

---

b

2. a $\frac{2}{6}$ and $\frac{1}{3}$ d $\frac{2}{8}$ and $\frac{1}{4}$
   b $\frac{4}{8}$ and $\frac{1}{2}$ e $\frac{3}{6}$ and $\frac{1}{2}$
   c $\frac{2}{4}$ and $\frac{1}{2}$ f $\frac{5}{10}$ and $\frac{1}{2}$

Page 24

1. $\frac{7}{7} = 1$ 6. $\frac{12}{14} = \frac{6}{7}$
2. $\frac{3}{6} = \frac{1}{2}$ 7. $\frac{3}{8}$
3. $\frac{3}{4}$ 8. $\frac{1}{7}$
4. $\frac{10}{15} = \frac{2}{3}$ 9. $\frac{6}{18} = \frac{1}{3}$
5. $\frac{5}{9}$ 10. $\frac{6}{12} = \frac{1}{2}$

Page 25

1. a 12   e 18   i 26
   b 31   f 25   j 25
   c 43   g 26   k 19
   d 9   h 23   l 15

2. a

8	
14	6
26	12	18

b

3	
14	11
21	7	18

c

8	
21	13
27	6	19

d

9	
15	6
18	3	9

Page 26

1. a 25p, 32p, 11p
   b 40p, 75p, 15p
   c £1 and 50p, £2 and 20p, £3 and 10p

2. a 80p   b £9 and 80p
   c T-shirt and socks
   d £7 and 80p

Page 27

1. a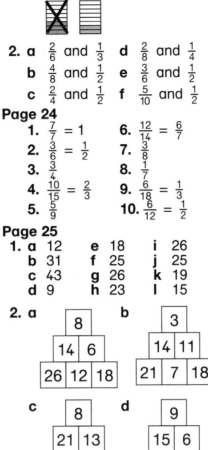

b

2. a west   c east
   b south   d west

Page 28

1. a 4.12   c 12.26
   b 10.38   d 5.34
   e   g
   f   h

2. a 35 minutes   c 40 minutes
   b 40 minutes   d 55 minutes

Page 29

1. a Joe   d 4
   b 7   e Mark and Laura
   c 3

Page 30

1.

74	46	108	94	114	136	28	150	96
102	85	77	109	192	59	261	395	128
314	61	100	205	116	299	94	105	306
108	93	209	183	318	417	89	101	200
52	74	82	211	260	300	192	245	412
112	196	418	309	234	108	386	193	350
376	190	210	106	92	34	76	84	272

You can see the odd number 99

2. a 16   e 14   i 11
   b 8   f 16   j 19
   c 20   g 28   k 17
   d even   h even   l odd
Answers a–h coloured blue
Answers i–l coloured red

Page 31

1. 200 + 50 + 1, two hundred and fifty-one,

736, seven hundred and thirty-six,

464, 400 + 60 + 4, four hundred and sixty-four

976, 900 + 70 + 6,

2. a 6
   b 346, 364, 436, 463, 634, 643

Page 32

1. 60   6. 3
2. 660   7. 900
3. 606   8. 0
4. 16   9. 400
5. 666   10. 9

Page 33

1. 110   6. 1700
2. 60   7. 1600
3. 80   8. 90
4. 1400   9. 70
5. 500   10. 1300

Page 34

1. 168   6. £1 and 20p
2. 274   7. 40
3. 372   8. 4
4. 242   9. £1 and 74p
5. 932   10. £2 and 90p

Page 35

1. hexagon
2. pentagon
3. quadrilateral
4. octagon
5. triangle
6.   7.
8.   9.
10.

Page 36
1. 93   6. 952
2. 152   7. 401
3. 711   8. 808
4. 670   9. 1009
5. 419   10. 714

Page 37
1. 40   6. 33
2. 18   7. 40
3. 60   8. 14
4. 35   9. 45
5. 8   10. 48

Page 38
1. £10 and 15p
2. £15 and 30p
3. £30 and 55p
4. £20 and 65p
5. £12 and 50p
6. £5 and 50p
7. £2 and 25p
8. £1 and 20p
9. 75p
10. £12 and 50p

Page 39
1. $\frac{2}{6}$ and $\frac{1}{3}$
2. $\frac{4}{8}$ and $\frac{2}{4}$ or $\frac{1}{2}$
3. $\frac{4}{8}$ and $\frac{2}{4}$ or $\frac{1}{2}$
4. $\frac{2}{4}$ and $\frac{1}{2}$
5. $\frac{3}{9}$ and $\frac{1}{3}$
6. 8 squares coloured
7. 4 squares coloured
8. 14 squares coloured
9. 15 squares coloured
10. 2 squares coloured

Page 40
1. 30 minutes
2. 20 minutes
3. 15 minutes
4. 5 minutes
5. 3 hours
6.
7.
8.
9.
10.

Page 41
1.
2.
3.
4.
5.
6.
7.
8.
9.
10.

Page 42
1. 74   6. 734
2. 88   7. 852
3. 10   8. 100
4. 10   9. 636
5. 10   10. 153

Page 43
1. 376   6. 999
2. 179   7. 923
3. 861   8. 990
4. 623   9. 1031
5. 788   10. 779

Page 44
1. 4   6. 5
2. 18   7. 40p
3. 6   8. 10
4. 80   9. 40
5. 10   10. 10p

Page 45
1. prism
2. not a prism
3. not a prism
4. prism
5. prism
6. not a prism
7. prism
8. prism
9. prism
10. prism

Page 46
1. 75 cm
2. 2000 g
3. 2000 m
4. 500 ml
5. 20 mm
6. 30 minutes
7. 45 minutes
8. 15 minutes
9. 30 seconds
10. 45 seconds

Page 47
1. 631 641 651 661
2. 489 389 289 189
3. 58 68 78 88
4. 69 59 49 39
5. 655 755 855 955
6. odd
7. odd
8. not odd
9. not odd
10. odd

Page 48
1. 300   6. 45
2. £150 7. £12
3. 160 cm 8. 33 cm
4. 240 m 9. 12 kg
5. 30p   10. 25p

Page 49
1. £1 and 70p
2. £2 and 05p
3. £3 and 10p
4. £1 and 01p
5. £2 and 07p
6. 754p   9. 912p
7. 207p   10. 177p
8. 349p

Page 50
1. 3   6. 6
2. 14   7. 16
3. 6   8. 14
4. 4   9. 24
5. 4   10. 27

Page 51
1. Jenny
2. Ravi
3. Road
4. Avenue
5. Lane
6. George, Lucy, Peter
7. February, April, November
8. 480g 635g 755g
9. Lee, Eric, Sandra
10. $\frac{1}{2}$ minute
    35 seconds
    1 minute

Page 52
1. 7.24 am
2. 5.05 pm
3. 6.15 am
4. 7.25 pm
5. 1.50 pm
6. 1.35 am

	12-hour digital clock	24-hour digital clock
7.		
8.	1.30 pm	09:45
9.	9.45 am	13:30
10.	6.15 pm	19:20
	7.20 pm	18:15

Page 53
1. 905   6. 364
2. 531   7. 68
3. 326   8. 79
4. 592   9. 319
5. 218   10. 407

Page 54
1. £1 and 38p
2. £1 and 88p
3. 63p
4. £1 and 73p
5. 92p
6. 10p
7. 61p
8. 28p
9. 4p
10. 40p

Page 55
1.   2.
3.   4.
5.
6. not a right angle
7. right angle
8. right angle
9. not a right angle
10. not a right angle

Page 56
1. 0.7   6. 0.1
2. 1.5   7. 0.3
3. 3.3   8. 0.5
4. 0.9   9. 0.7
5. 2.4   10. 0.9

Page 57
1. 6   3. 14
2. 8   4. 26
5. 17
6. 8 remainder 2
7. 14 remainder 1
8. 11 remainder 3
9. 15 remainder 2
10. 8 remainder 6

Page 58
1. 12.00
2. 8.45
3. 11.55
4. 1.15
5. 12.20
6. 35 minutes
7. £2 and 98p
8. 56p
9. 2.30 pm
10. 70

Page 59
1. 108   6. 159
2. 164   7. 168
3. 106   8. 268
4. 141   9. 222
5. 224   10. 295

Page 60
1. Thursday
2. Wednesday
3. Sunday
4. 5
5. 9
6. 26th December
7. Sunday
8. 2nd December
9. 12th
10. January

Page 61
1. 25
2. 5
3. 20
4. 25
5. 45
6. 10
7. 10
8. football
9. basketball
10. 75